For tutorials, Partner Dance demonstrations, and Dance Party videos,

visit:

jonathanreok.com

Rhythm Rhythm Revolution
Dance Puzzles for Rhythmic Literacy
Book 1 - The Basics   by Jonathan Reök

© 2019 Jonathan Reök
All rights reserved   Printed in USA
ISBN 978-0-578-59267-1

Reök Publishing
Minneapolis, MN USA

Cover design by Darryl Drozdik
darryldrozdikdesign.com

GAME RULES

In order to pass a level you must first answer these questions:

    1. What is the time signature?

    2. What does that *mean*?

    3. How do you conduct that time signature?

Then dance the level. All these elements must be performed simultaneously:

    1. March the beat (one step per beat).

    2. Say the rhythm.

    3. Slap top-line notes with the right hand on the right leg.

    4. Slap top-line rests with the right hand on the *left* shoulder.

    5. Slap bottom-line notes with left hand on the left leg.

    6. Slap bottom-line rests with the left hand on the *right* shoulder.

    - Slaps must be held for the entire duration of the note or rest. (e.g. For a half note in 4/4 time, slap the leg and hold for an entire two beats. If the hand lifts after one beat, *you're **disqualified.*** Try again. ツ Ties extend the duration of the note. (e.g. for a half note tied to a quarter note in 4/4 time, hold for three beats.)

Then play the level on your instrument - first the top line (if applicable) through the entire level and then the bottom line (if applicable) through the entire level. Then pianists and other polyphonic instrumentalists play both lines.

CHALLENGE LEVELS may be performed by a group of four (or more) players - one conducting, one dancing, one performing the top line on their instrument, and one performing the bottom line on their instrument. Then rotate roles until every player has performed each role.

HINT: In order to pass a level, you may want to first use DEEP PRACTICE techniques: practice in s l o w motion, practice one element at a time (just one hand at a time or just the feet or just the words). After you've built the skills *slowly* and *separately*, then put the dance back together again (feet, both hands, voice) and increase the tempo.

★1

★2

★3

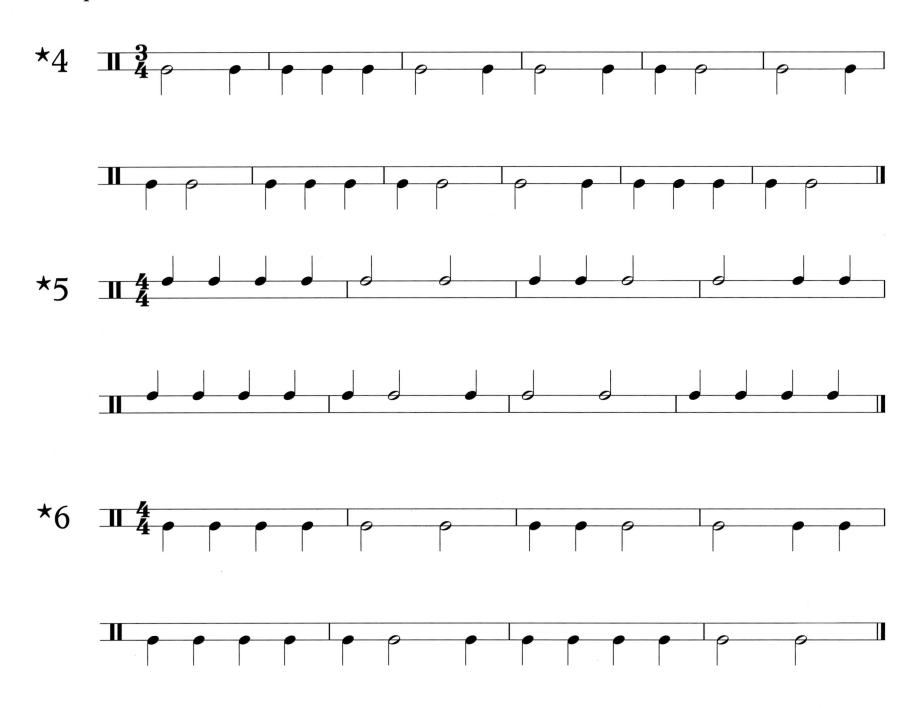

★19

★20

★21

10

★31

★32

Challenge Level

★33

18

Challenge Level

★42

Dance Party mix #1
(Repeat each section as you choose to fit your soundtrack.)

Partner Dance mix #1
(Repeat each section to your heart's content.)

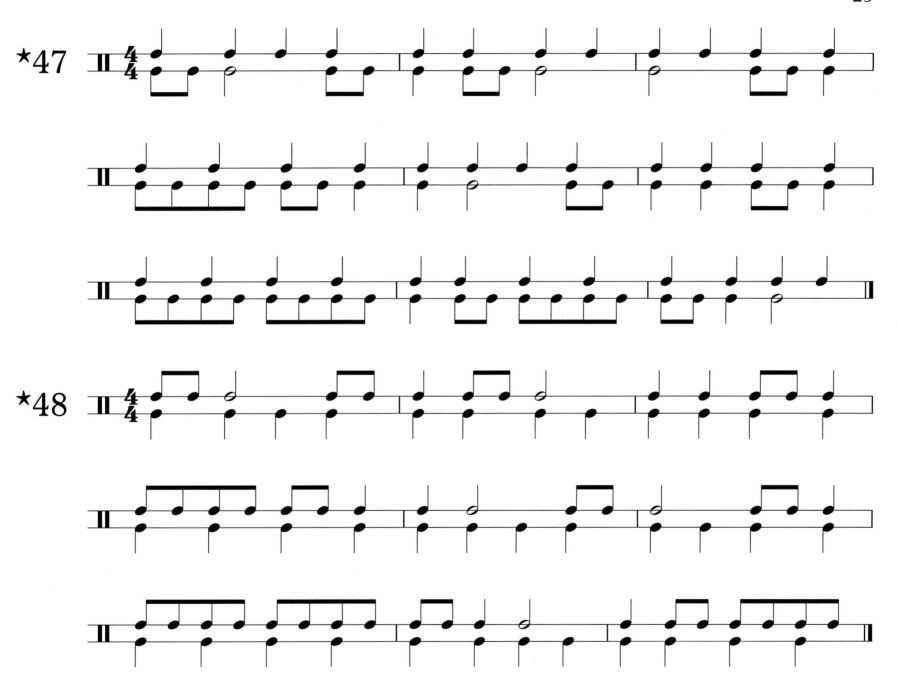

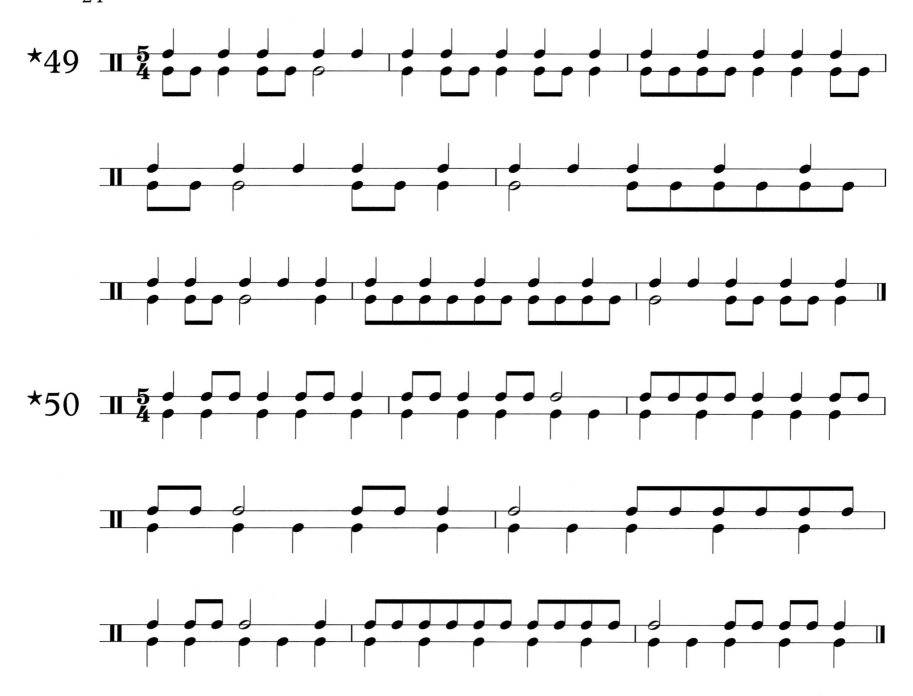

*51

*52

26

Challenge Level

★59

32

★64

★65

★66

★67

Challenge Level

★68

Dance Party mix #2

(Repeat each section as you choose to fit your soundtrack.)

36

Partner Dance mix #2
(Repeat each section to your heart's content.)

42

44

Challenge Level

★85

Challenge Level

★94

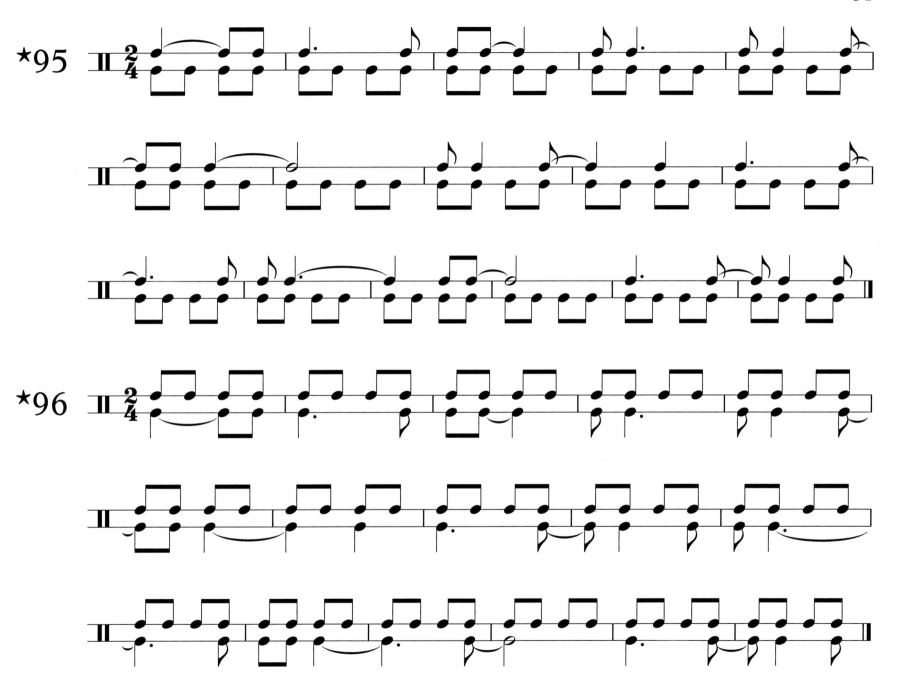

52

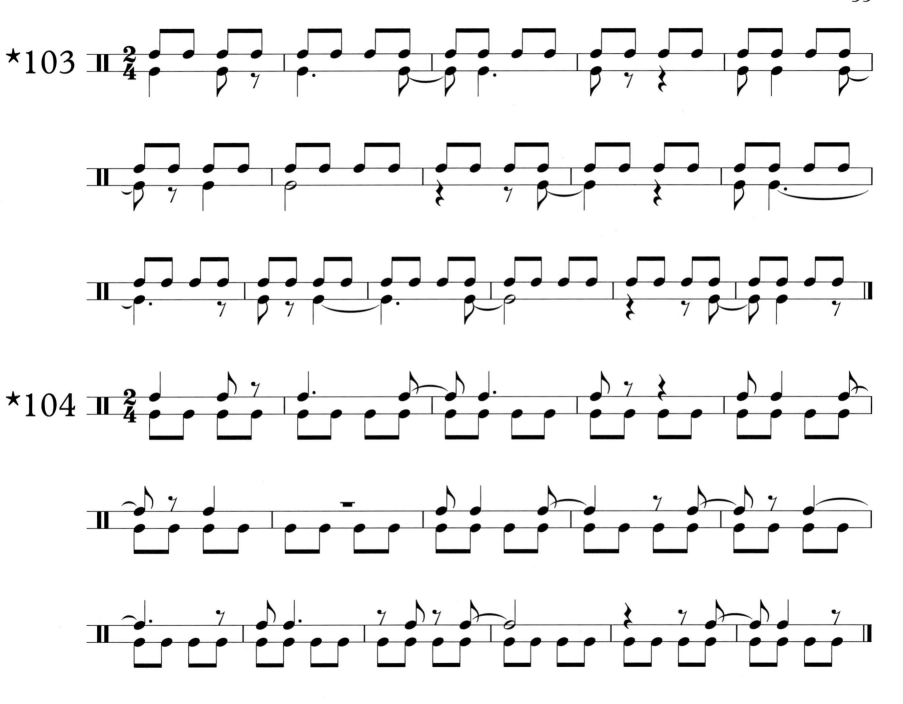

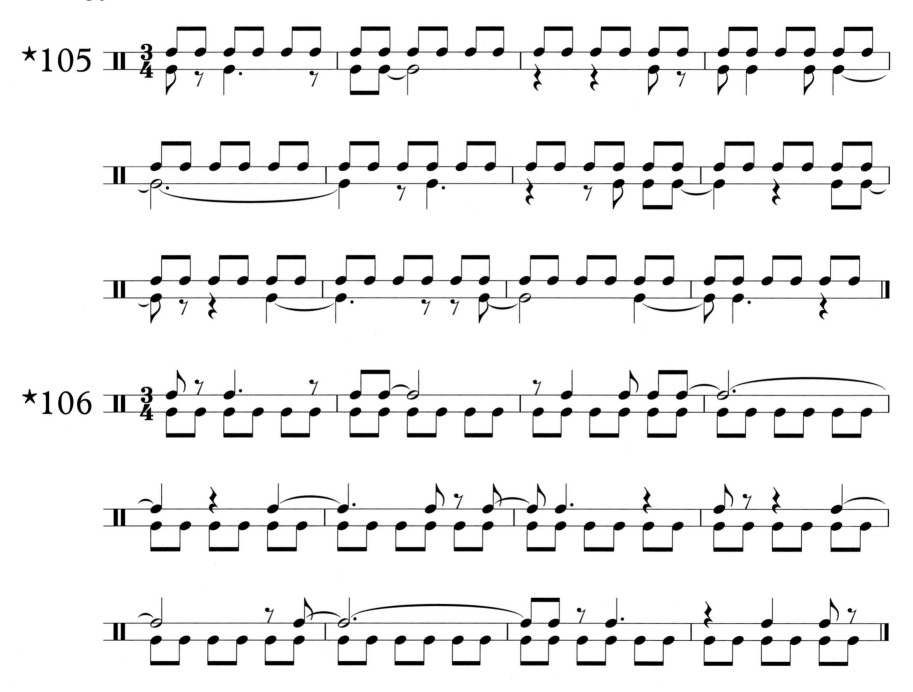

58

Challenge Level

★111

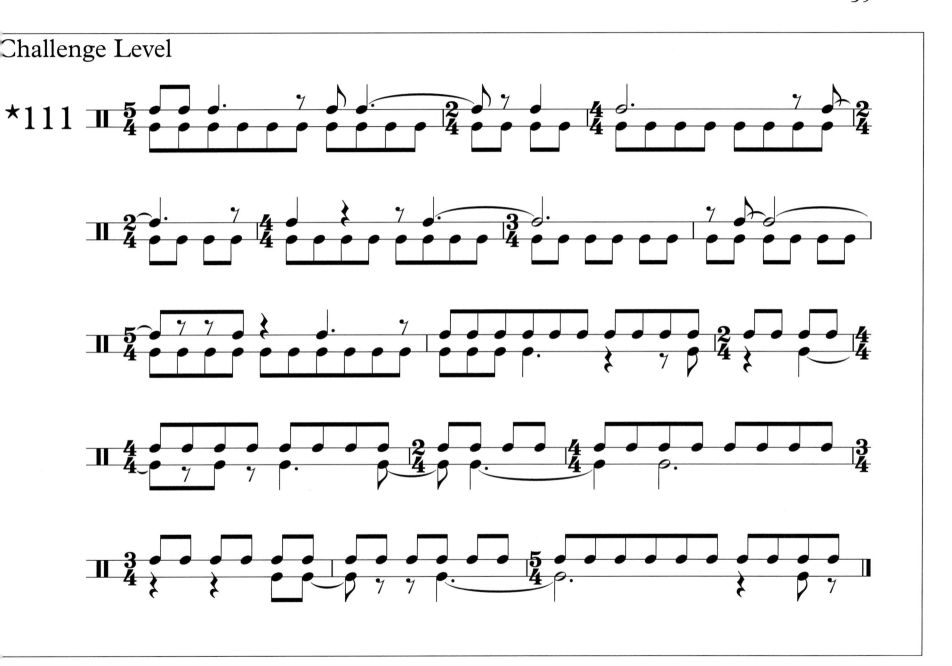

60

★114

★115

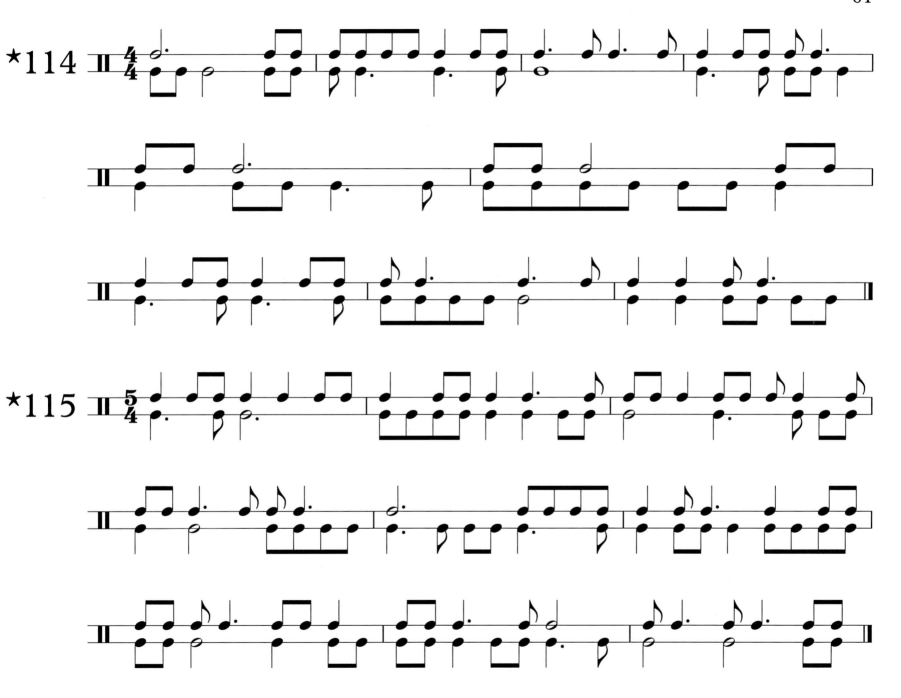

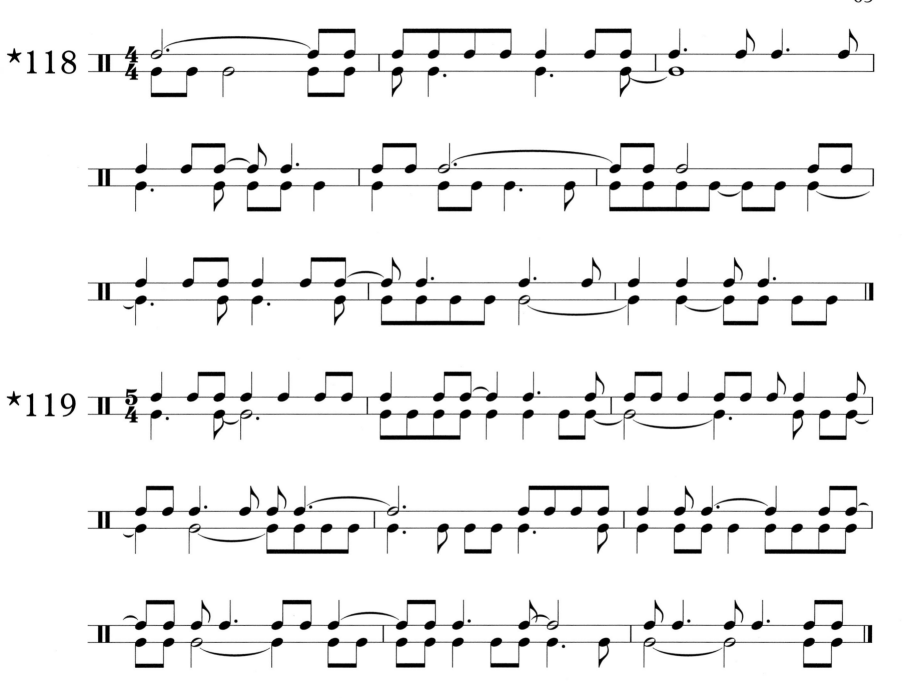

65

66

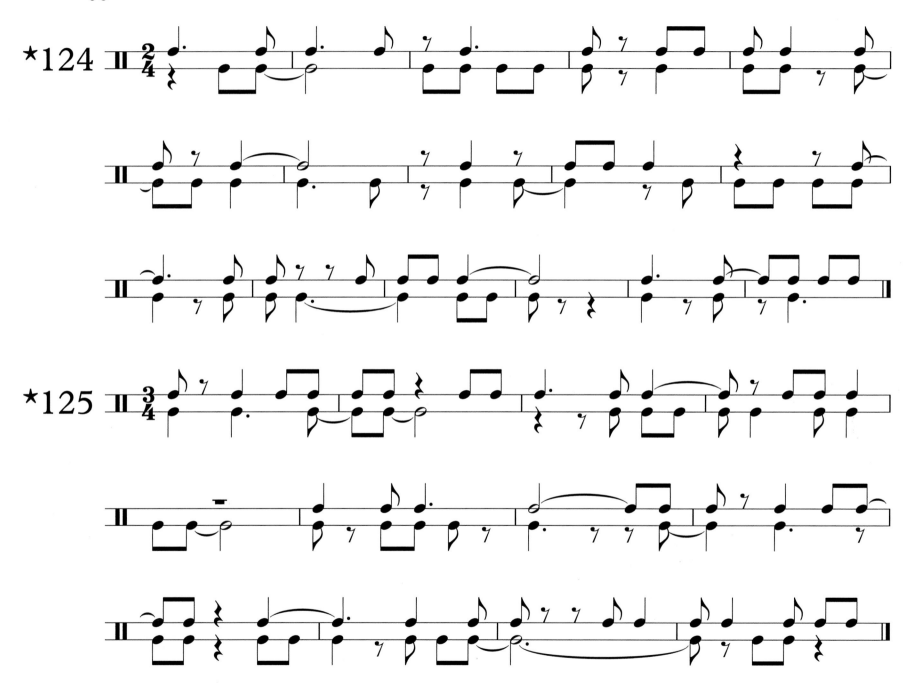

68

Challenge Level

⋆128

Dance Party mix #3

(Repeat each section as you choose to fit your soundtrack.)

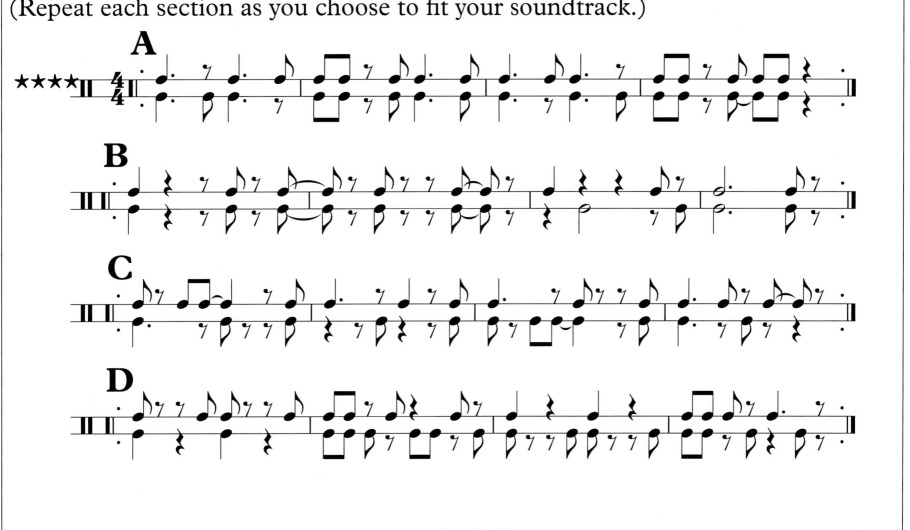

Partner Dance mix #3
(Repeat each section to your heart's content.)

72

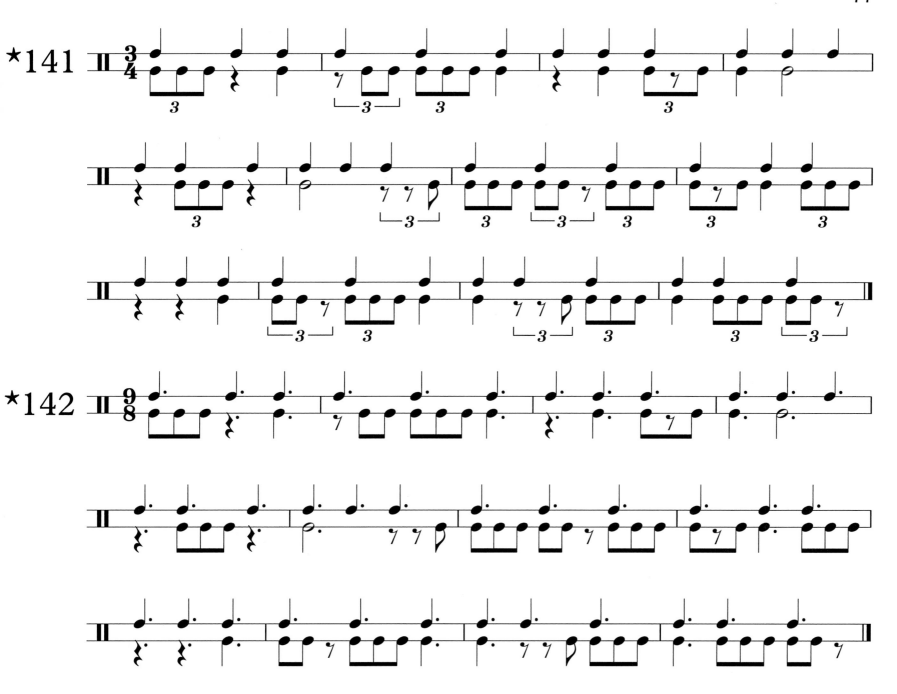

★141

★142

Challenge Level

★145

82

84

Challenge Level

★154

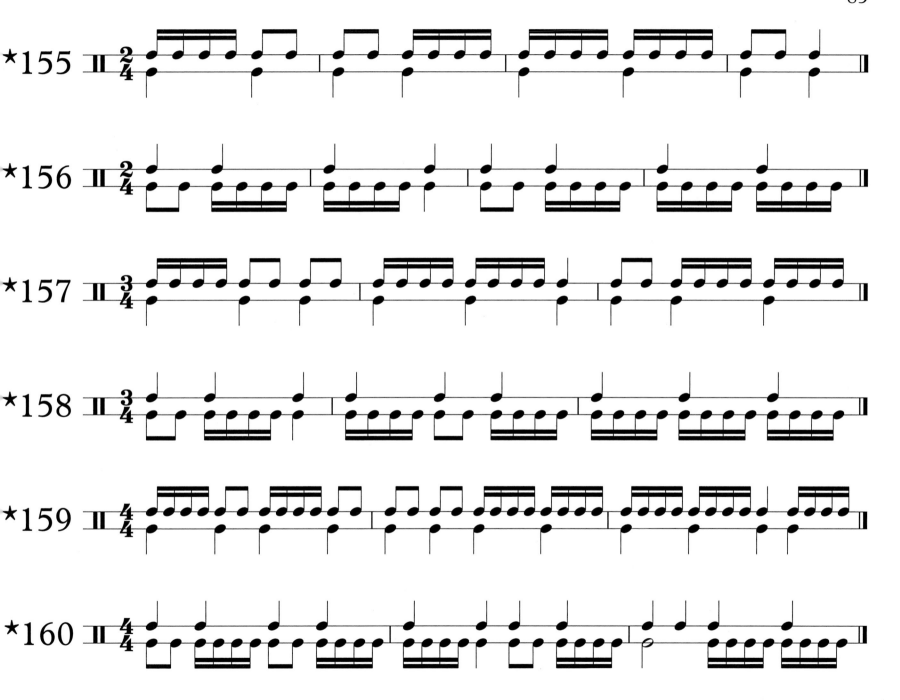

86

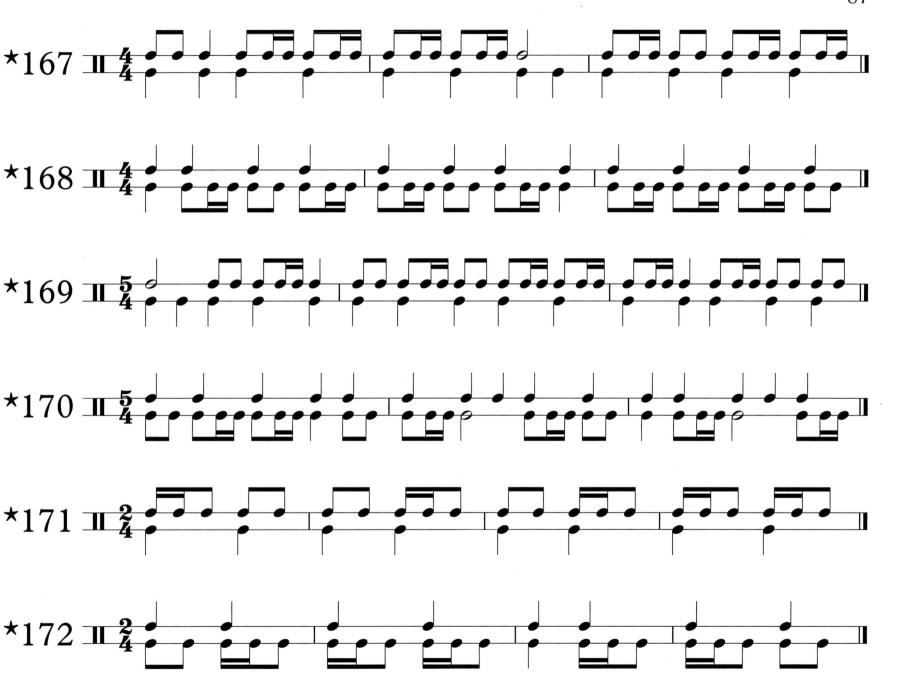

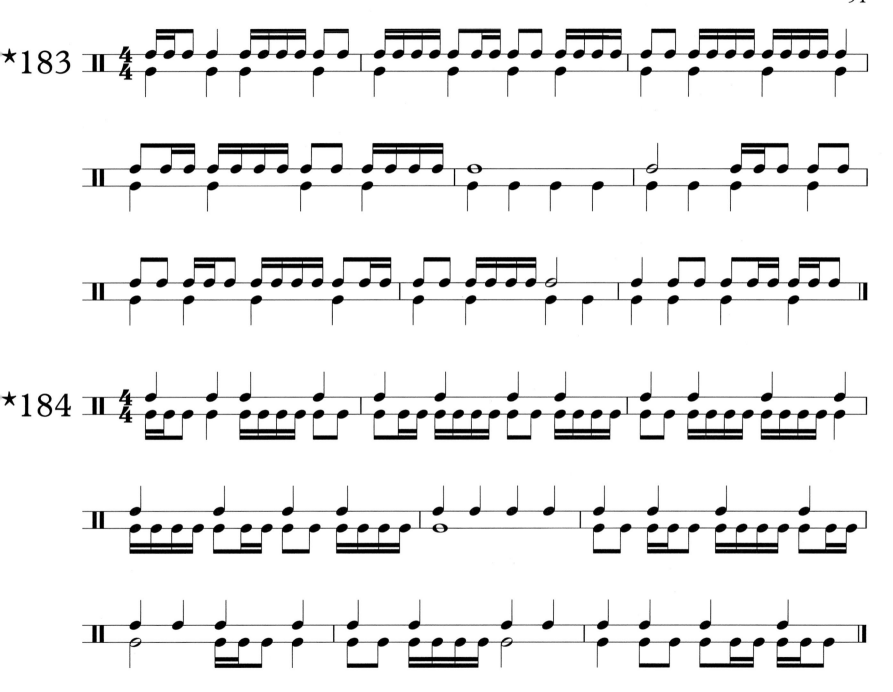

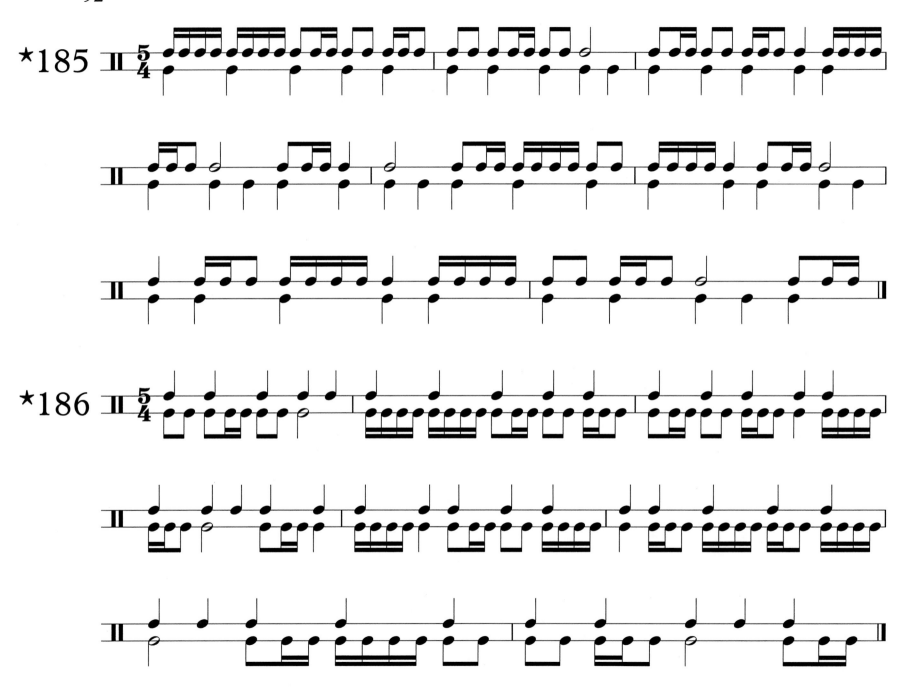

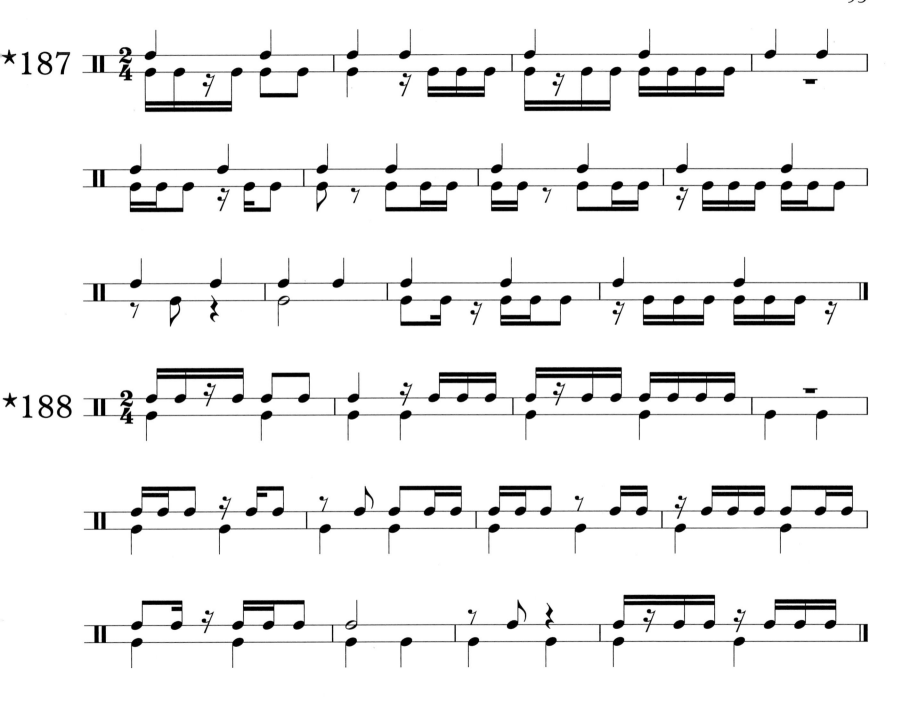

Challenge Level

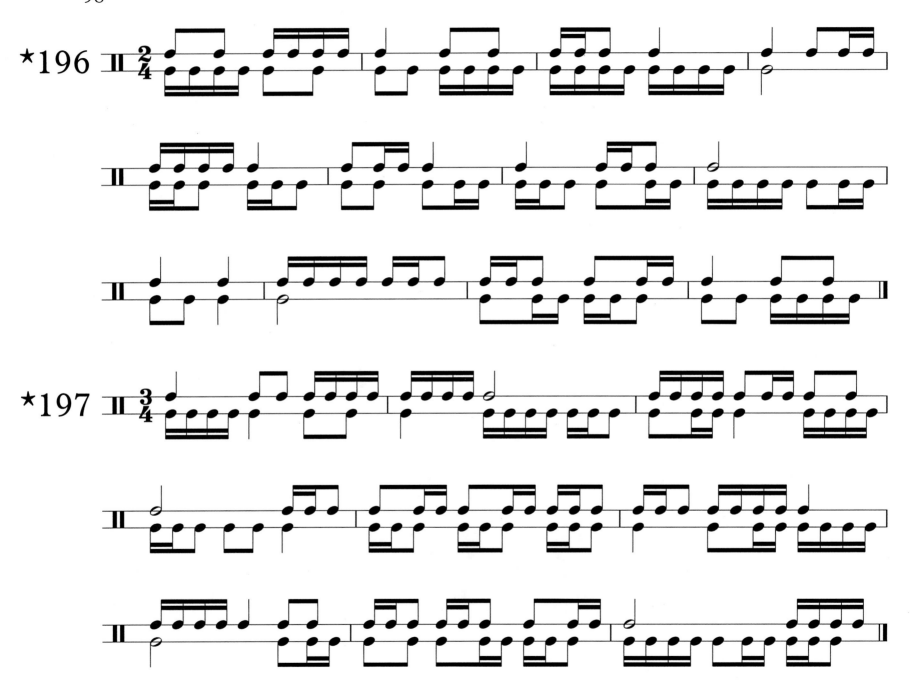

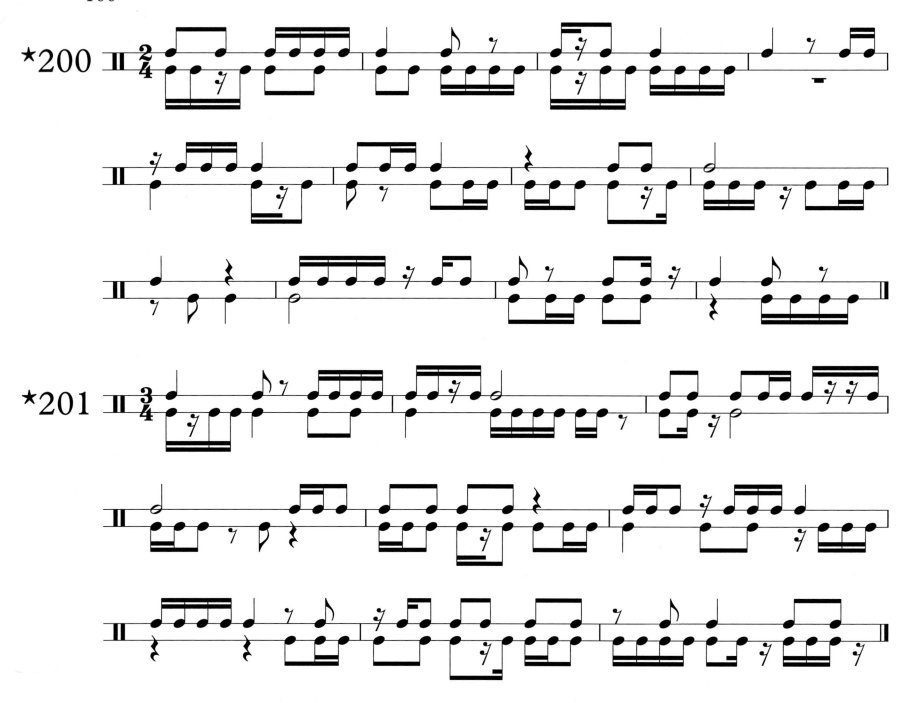

Challenge Level

★204

★205

Dance Party mix #4 (Repeat each section as you choose to fit your soundtrack.)

Partner Dance mix #4
(Repeat each section to your heart's content.)